A MAGIC TIME

and other

POEMS

A MAGIC TIME

and other

POEMS

Carol Boxall

Carol Ann Boxall

A

Published by Armitage Publications.
1 Manor Road, Abbotskerswell, Newton Abbot, TQ12 5PR

ISBN   978-0-9565680-0-7

Printed and bound by Short Run Press Ltd., Exeter, Devon.

A donation from the sale of this book will be given to
The Alzheimer's Research Trust

CONTENTS

To
Mayfield friends, who without their prompting and encouragement, this book would never have got started, and to David for his technical help and advice.

START A POEM

Writing thoughts down on a page
Will get them in perspective,
Then you can be selective
And make ideas effective,
By writing them with pen and ink,
It helps one with another link,
This often happens in a blink
To start a poem.

Safely keep notes on a page,
Thinking of a special rhyme
May take quite a lot of time,
For achievement, let thoughts climb,
As with a cryptic puzzle`s clues
The answer`s there, look hard, then choose,
You really have nothing to lose
So start a poem.

With fresh paper, a new page,
You`ll find the motivation,
And great determination
Then, with results, elation!
Joyful thoughts, with happiness found
In lines of rhyme, rhythm and sound,
And if like me you feel spellbound,
Then, write a poem.

THE PEN

An open page, invites the pen
To pause, then start to write again.

A story flows, as does the ink,
Pen really has no time to think,
Finding the words just tumble on,
To stay like night, when day has gone.
Each is precisely written down,
Portrayed with smiles, or with a frown.
One may be strange, another dear,
Interpretations though are clear.
A spelling or grammar mistake
The careful pen would never make.
Written words spread, filling the page,
Where paper holds them, in her cage.

Turnover, hidden now from view,
Will words remain unchanged and true?

Turn back the page once more, and read,
Cementing words, with thought and need.
New page, prepare, reveal yourself,
Let pen become a prancing elf.
This freshly opened page invites
Excitingly creative flights.
Given more room, to move and feel,
Pen lightly skips a Scottish reel.
As words pour forth in fading light
Pen will write on into the night,
He cannot rest, ink could be spilled!
Another page will soon be filled.

("What do you think, Woody?")

IMAGINE IF...

Imagine if the sky was green,
And all the grass was blue.
Imagine if birds couldn`t fly,
And so, we humans flew.

We wouldn`t need a motor car
To get from A to B,
Or ferry boats, or a cruise ship,
We`d fly across the sea.

We wouldn`t have to wait and queue
To catch a country bus,
Saving time, we`d quickly fly home,
That way, there`d be no fuss.

We wouldn`t have to catch a train
To Birmingham, or Crewe,
And definitely wouldn`t ask
The porter what to do!

We wouldn`t have to ride a bike,
Or push it up a hill,
Drifting high, we`d catch the thermals,
Our arms, as wings, held still.

We wouldn`t worry if it rained,
Or have to wear a Mac,
For, like a bird, we`d give a shake,
While rain fell off our back!

Just think, what pleasure it would be
To fly just anywhere,
A little jump, feet off the ground,
Gliding, without a care.

Imagine looking down upon
A field of brightest blue,
And looking up to green sky, but,
What would the poor birds do?

SHAPES

Whilst dawning hours tick slowly by,
Sinister shapes in shadows lie,
How dark, how threatening shapes seem
Not caught by glow of moon's last beam.

The shape that worries one the most,
Is hanging on the carved bedpost!
Real, turns into surreal at night,
Remaining, till dark turns to light.

Outlined, before the wake of day,
Patiently trying to delay
The morning's birth, strangely unknown,
Only by daylight colours shown.

Like dormant statues, shaped in wood,
Seen often, now misunderstood,
Unchanging, they do not pretend
To being other than a friend.

But were they there the night before,
Or did they walk in through the door.
Scared, unsure, we can`t be certain
So we check, behind each curtain!

THE ROOM

I floated through the window,

There wasn`t any door,

The cloth was on the ceiling,

The dinner on the floor.

I lifted up the teapot

Fresh milk flowed from the spout.

If I turned the hot tap on

Would tea come pouring out?

Shelves were hanging upside down,

Plus cups and saucers too,

Plates were spinning on the walls.

How could all this be true?

I found some bread and butter

That turned into a cake!

Just as I began to eat

I found myself awake!

A HOUSEWIFE'S LOT

She gets up every morning, and then wakes the others up,
She pours out all the orange juice, before she gets a cup,
She cooks the breakfast, clears away and does the washing-up.
A housewife's lot is such a busy one, busy one!

She makes the beds, changing the sheets, hangs washing in the sun,
Gets out the Hoover, cleans the floor and some may think this fun!
She washes windows, scrubs the bath, then gets the shopping done.
A housewife's lot is such a busy one, busy one!

If raining hard, she rushes home to get the washing in,
Then spills the milk and cleans it up, puts rubbish in the bin.
To sit down for five minutes now, would surely be a sin!
A housewife's lot is such a busy one, etc!

She picks some apples off the tree, and makes an apple pie,
She cooks the dinner, clears away, washing and wiping dry,
Then someone falls and hurts their knee and soon begins to cry.
OOH! A housewife's lot is such a busy one, etc!

The next day brings another set of jobs that she must do,
And one that's always cropping up is cleaning out the loo!
You know that phrase, a woman's work, I'm telling you, it's TRUE!
A housewife's lot is never ever done, ever done!

(After Gilbert and Sullivan's)
(A policeman's lot is not a happy one.)
If you sing the last line of each verse
The work gets done quicker!

THE DAY BEGINS

The day begins with quiet calm,
Limp leaves hang silently,
Mist rises lazily
From damp, dew laden grass.
Strangely, birds are restless.

The sunless sun rose earlier,
A soft sulphurous light
Covers fields in our sight,
A rustling sound is heard,
From the holly`s sharp leaves.

Enormous raindrops fall,
Forerunners of a storm,
Swiftly large puddles form.
Scotch pines sway heavily,
As the rain thunders down.

Gathering speed, winds blow fiercely,
Trees bend mercilessly,
Grey visibility.
Now daytime night descends,
Silver tipped rivers rage.

Dying trees are brought to their knees,
The storms intensity
Has grown ferociously,
Branches fly through the air,
All life must shelter now.

Next day,
Plants lie flattened into new shapes,
Small weak stems have their ripped roots bare.
Baby rabbits, sniffing the air
Realising the storm has passed,
Seek food, in desolate safety.

SNOWDROP

Your dress pure white, with frill of green,
Neatly folded away, unseen,
We glance, no sign, next day you`re here
Small snowdrop, first bulb of the year.

Through wintry darkened, shortened days,
This never ceases to amaze,
Your long awaited great surprise
Grows, with the sun and clear blue skies.

When daylight fades, with sharpened air,
It lends a bed of frost to share.
We find your dress and tiny face
With patterns formed, as if from lace.

Then snowflakes may decide to fall,
But you`ve grown safely by the wall
Protected from big drifts of snow,
As only you snowdrop, would know.

Now searching for you, once again,
Your pretty dress is washed with rain,
Which gives it quite a magic sheen,
Small snowdrop, edged with frill of green.

SPRING

Yellow stars, amid the green
In the distance, hardly seen.
Closer, in confusions throng
Hear their individual song.

Some will turn, they are so shy,
Looking down with hidden eye,
Others, boldly face the breeze,
Knowing they are sure to please.

Newly opened, golden, bright,
Proudly filled with morning light.
Daffodils, as Wordsworth knew,
Seen by him, now seen by you.

Petals shining, so serene,
In fields, `neath trees, in-between
Their branches bent, dipping low,
Seen, reflecting sunlight`s glow.

Beauty that will surely bring
Glowing warmth, to coolest Spring.

AUNT MAUD'S HOLIDAY

At Easter Aunt Maud wrote to say,
I`d really like to come and stay.
At once we answered, with a plan,
And so her holiday began.

Maud`s friend drove her halfway, to Mere,
Whilst we drove there, then back to here.
We`d piled her luggage on the rack,
With more, plus me, stowed in the back.

I wondered where we`d put it all,
Her bedroom, adequate but small,
But when unpacked, it fitted in,
So Aunt Maud`s stay could now begin.

That night Aunt Maud slept like a log,
She didn`t even hear our dog.
When daylight came, it wasn`t long
Before she broke forth into song.

The clothes she wore for going out
On holiday to gadabout,
Were brightly flowered flowing frocks,
With matching shoes, and ankle socks.

Adorned in such unusual wear,
Quite often, people stopped to stare.
So colourful, she`d cause a stir,
We didn`t mind, it was, just her!

We liked the way she wore her hat,
Fixed firmly, with a gentle pat.
If clouds appeared, and rain came down,
Umbrella up, she`d laugh, not frown.

One morning, at the Easter fair
She walked about without a care,
Holding a bag, that weighed a ton,
Which, just like her brimmed full of fun.

Maud`s favourite place was Paignton Zoo,
The reason why? Well here`s a clue,
The animals amazing ways
Fulfilled her photographic craze.

She loved the view from Shaldon`s Ness,
And shopped in Torquay and Totnes,
Gifts, souvenirs, carefully bought
For friends, of whom she often thought.

Too soon the time was drawing near
For us to drive her back to Mere.
No room for me this time, for sure,
Her presents took my space, and more!

I said I didn`t really mind,
I`d be content to stay behind.
Three hugs, two waves, one beep of horn.
They disappeared. I was forlorn.

Later on, Maud wrote a letter
Saying, "I feel so much better,
Oh, how the time with you just flew,
I miss you so."
We miss her too.

13

WILD COLOUR

Mauve violets found at our feet
With tiny scented faces, greet
Each other, as they grow.

Scarlet pimpernels will abound
On any unattended ground,
In miniature delight.

Blue speedwell hurries through the lawn,
Lying low whilst grass is shorn,
To reappear unharmed.

White daises too somehow survive
The cutting blade, staying alive,
Ringed petals gaily bright.

Gold buttercups stand upright, tall,
In clusters by the garden wall,
Reflecting sunny light.

Each Spring their seeds will grow again
Freely sown, well watered by rain,
Giving us, wild colour.

THE SEED

I`m germinating, thought the seed,

Splitting her sides with laughter.

Her roots grew down,

Her stem grew up,

Bright flowers came, soon after!

The flowers opened, petals shone,

Bursting with their importance.

Soon they were picked,

Driven away,

Bunched up and sold, for four pence!

A lady brought the flowers home,

Perfume filled every corner.

But she fell sick,

And died alone,

Just flowers left, to mourn her.

BLOSSOM

Oh so gentle is the breeze,
Lovingly, the earth receives
Blossom, falling from the trees,
Feather light, without a sound
Floating softly to the ground,
Snowy petals gather round.

Patterns made in dappled sun,
Countless numbers, one by one
Wonder, "Is our work now done?"
"Yes, having attracted bees,
Your work, plus their expertise,
Pollinated all the trees."
"Now, stay resting where you fell,
Sleep, whilst fruit begins to swell."

Ripe fruit plays a vital part
As nourishment, at its heart
Dormant seeds lie, soon to start
Growing, this wonder is true,
But from many just a few
Seeds, will germinate anew.

MAY GARDEN

The strong winds blow
Blossom, like snow,
Beneath the apple tree,
Grass grows so fast,
Poor mower`s last
To come in, for his tea.

Sweet Brompton Stocks
Perfume, unlocks
Our eyes to see its show,
Bright glowing pink
Flowered stems, link
With seed pods, as they grow.

Forget-me-nots
Self seed and lots
Spread freely, far and wide.
A lovely hue,
A sea of blue,
So named, they cannot hide.

Pruned roses, bare
And bloomless, stare
Down, by the sunken lawn.
Another tune
We`ll hear in June,
When buds burst forth at dawn.

Cowslips now fade
In meadow made
With grass left longer there.
By willow's side
Young children hide
And seek, without a care.

CAMELLIA

Camellia, whose wondrous sight,
With rarity, is borne
On coloured particles of light,
To which our eyes are drawn.

From glossy leaves, tight buds will burst,
Unveiling all that's new,
One, to uniquely open first
Shows blossom, peeping through.

Uncurled, fresh petals new array
Soon turn, to face cool sun,
Bringing completion, their display
Of symmetry, well done.

A DOG ROSE

It`s said a dog is man`s best friend,

And, nine times out of ten that`s true,

But should he need

To have a feed,

Just watch your plate`s not licked clean too!

SUMMER ARRIVES

Summer arrives, June scented
Warm air caressing my skin.
Roses scramble over walls,
Pale pink petals, paper thin.

Busy bees, seeking nectar
Crawl in crevices, to find
Blue campanulas and start
Sipping, sucking, till they`ve dined.

Wildly trailed wisteria
Spreads atop the tall fir tree,
Changing green to misty mauve,
Creating new scenery.

Pigeons keep disappearing
Deep within this tangled haze,
Well hidden nests they`re guarding,
From the magpies beady gaze.

Swallows dive in azure waves,
Acrobatics shown compare
With swifts, both catch small insects
In Summer`s cool evening air.

A MAGIC TIME

Whilst sunshine warms with scattered rays
Mosaic butterfly displays,
Watch wings spread wide.
When dry, they fly
Through softly disappearing sky.

Sad moment with such brilliance gone,
As if the sun had never shone.
Then seen, sublime,
A magic time
From nature's jewelled pantomime.

So butterflies rest here awhile,
Your coloured wings prettily smile,
But when you go,
Fly to and fro,
Your wings will then a spectrum show.

SILK THREADS

xx

Silk stitches sit crossed legged in rows,
Placed tightly side by side,
Smiling, they chat, as each one knows
They`re to each other tied.

xxx

They wait, another thread arrives
To join them in their row,
Smiling, they watch it, as it strives
To help the needle sew.

xxxx

Silk threads through cloth so gently glide,
Though cross stitch is their name,
Smiling, with neighbours either side
Sewn friends they will remain.

xxxxx

Their pattern neatly forms, petite,
Each thread stays in its place,
Smiling, positioning their feet
Not wanting room or space.

xxxxxx

Their colours blend together, planned
With pink shades next to blue,
Smiling, they clasp each other's hand,
Ending in stitches, too!

xxxxxxx

THE SHOW

Aunt Maud had always wanted
To act upon a stage,
Maybe to sing, or maybe dance,
Dancing was all the rage!

She met a group of actors
And asked to join their club,
Rehearsals were three days a week,
Held in a local pub.

The show was "Iolanthe,"
A fairy was her part,
And other members, even leads,
Were helpful from the start.

When practising the numbers
She worked extremely hard,
Learning her lines, and how to fly,
And flew, more than a yard!

Aunt Maud liked drinking cider,
It made her feel alive,
Increasing her deliverance
Of "Rock Around..." or jive!

One evening, Maud drank too much,
Disaster! Circling round
Her wings snapped suddenly and ouch!
She crashed down to the ground.

Her arms and legs hurt badly,
She tried to stand up straight,
Unsafe, she found her wounded legs
Just wouldn`t take her weight.

Maud felt so disappointed,
Yearning to be a pro,
However, it was not to be,
For her, there was no show.

Maud wrestled with her conscience.
Weeks later, free from pain,
She joined her friends, plus their new show,
But never drank again!

SUNSHINE

Rising sun,

Gently ease

Glowing rays

Between the trees.

Golden beams

Growing, still

Shining on

The window sill.

Sunshine, so

Comforting.

Shadows are

Now lengthening.

Setting sun,

Nearly gone.

Pillow pink,

To sleep upon.

DOVE

Sleep sweet dove
And dream of love,
Deep in thy down,
Thy snow white gown,
Curl thy head and make thy bed.
Sleep sweet dove
And dream of love.

Sleep sweet dove
With thy true love,
Soft is her down
Deep feathered gown,
Lay her head upon thy bed,
Dream sweet dove
With thy true love.

Wake sweet dove
Each day with love,
Deep is thy down
Like her pure gown,
Lift her soft head from thy bed,
Wake sweet dove
Then fly with love.

TO BE WED

Her fingers feel soft velvet folds
Pleasingly made, enlaced with gold`s,
While amber beads shine round her waist,
So gracefully she'll be embraced.

In contrast, crisp and dark attire
Is worn by him, who`ll be her sire.
Today, two lovers, to be wed,
Such eager love, will share their bed.

They meet and smile, a longing smile,
For they'll be wed, in just awhile.
Soft vows are said, as if one voice,
Assured they`ve made this wondrous choice.

Through wine and music`s throbbing tone,
They dearly long to be alone
To start their lives, now joined as one,
As twilight comes, and day is done.

His fingers feel the snowy sheet,
Her perfect form lain there to meet
With love, that she has longed to please,
A pleasure shared, now both can seize.

A SPECIAL DAY

A special day
A special night,
One is dark
One is light
A special dawn
A special eve,
One to stay
One to leave?

A special thought,
A special word,
One will speak
One has heard.
A special touch
A special smile,
One will stay,
For awhile.

A special love
A special kiss,
One will give.
One will miss.
A special look
A special sigh,
Not a sound.
No goodbye.

A FROZEN TEAR

As I lie still, cold winter`s air

Hangs silent, freezing my despair.

This coldest night will last a year,

For sadness is a frozen tear.

Small diamond yet set with a sigh,

Unloose your hold that I may cry.

Unfrozen then, will sadness go?

Will you return?

When will I know?

NATURE

A leaf flutters down,
Falling like her tears,
Slowly, without sound
So that no one hears,
Settling on the ground
Moist with dew and rain,
Others all around,
Interlaced are lain.

A bird flutters down,
New born from its nest,
Feathers and soft down
Falling from its breast.
Listen to the call,
Mother Nature's cry,
Softening its fall,
There in leaves to lie.

FORGIVE

Forgive the sun, for not shining
When shrouded by cumulus cloud.
Whilst hidden, it is still smiling,
With a warmth of which it is proud.

Forgive the rain for not falling
Gently, as a gardener needs
Just small amounts of showering,
Too much, can encourage the weeds!

Forgive the wind, for not blowing
As washing hangs limply to dry.
Then turning up at a wedding,
Making pretty hats fly sky high!

Forgive the fog, for appearing
To make our world vanish from view.
This mischievous prank, transforming
The scenery that we all knew.

Forgive the snow, for not coming,
As Christmas day promises fade.
Blizzards then start, without warning,
When long journeys have to be made!

Forgive us all, for not saying
"Thank you," to someone who tries.
Forgive us too, for not seeing
The beauty, in front of our eyes.

SWEET PEAS

Sweet Peas, washed by showers
At sunset, whose flowers
Form a palette of light
Painted pale mauve, to white.
Brushed with raindrops, a few
Purples will change to blue,
While the delicate cream
Ones, unaltered would seem.

Petals, sweetly scented,
Red too, represented,
Like small beacons on fire
Moving up through the wire,
Their curled buds alongside,
Where the ladybirds hide,
Camouflaged from our view,
Safe from predators too.

LONG FURROWS

Long furrows regimental rows
Hold secrets. Hidden well within
The warmth, permeating their soil,
Are seeds, whose growth will soon begin.

Edged by a hedge of wayside flowers,
This fringed red field, will grow to green.
Who holds the brush? What colour next?
Who paints this ever changing scene?

As we can miss a well known phrase
Repeated daily in a tune,
So beauty of a distant field
Goes unseen, should we blink too soon.

On that warm evening, knowing this,
We felt a longing to be free,
And in-between the furrows, walked
On red earth, reaching to the sea.

HAVE YOU?

Have you
Trudged miles through fields of stubble,
Found colours in a bubble,
Watched a peacock spread his tail,
Camped all night in rain and hail?

Have you
Seen a stag appear at dawn,
Raked the moss out of a lawn,
Grown your own horse chestnut tree,
Been stung by a bumble bee?

Have you
Felt the hot breath of a horse,
Learnt some Semaphore and Morse,
Fallen down a flight of stairs,
Travelled freely without fares?

Have you
Heard the late news bulletin,
Tried to play a mandolin,
Sailed at midnight on the sea,
Made a belt in macramé?

Have you
Slept and left a book unread,
Helped a rabbit shape his bed,
Patched up socks and trousers torn,
Often risen before dawn?

Have you
Dodged the wings of flying bats,
Knitted jumpers, scarves and hats,
Seen Van Gogh`s "Sunflowers" art,
Cooked a jam and treacle tart?

Have you
Sewed Christmas sequinned glitter
Helped to clear foreshore litter,
Hunted tadpoles in a pond,
Danced with fairies and a wand?

Have you
Viewed the eclipse of the sun
Raced a hundred yards and won,
Known a new born babies cry,
Borne a difficult goodbye?

HONESTY

Outside is eerie stillness,
A yellow light brings calm.
Poor weary willow weighed by thought,
Has fronds hung down, like palm.

Indoors, spread wide and upright,
Dried honesty stands tall,
Transparent shining discs, which watch
Round raindrops start to fall.

One or two, then hundreds more
Cascading, pierce the ground,
Innumerable they gather strength
Whilst thunder rumbles round.

Oval discs, silkily smooth
With faces pale as ash,
Watch darts of electricity,
Followed by thunders crash.

When frightening sheets of lightning
Streak right across the sky,
Persistent rain lashes down, but
Brave honesty stays dry.

37

ROUND BERRIES

Round berries hang in Autumn`s air,
Each having equal rights to share
Their ripened warmth, their rosy glare,
With anyone who stops to stare.

Two pigeons fly through Autumn`s air,
A small branch takes their weight, with care.
Rich berries relished, such choice fare,
Both feast, until their branch is bare.

Dark clouds shed rain in Autumn`s air.
A sudden storm hits, fair and square.
Leaves shower down. Will wild winds tear
Red berries from this pigeon pair?

When clouds have passed, and Autumn`s air
Is calm again, I go to where
The pigeons fed. I find them there
Peacefully preening, unaware.

THE HORSE CHESTNUT

The old horse chestnut`s trunk, shows girth
Grown wider during years since birth.
Such strength now spreads out into six
Arms, tapering to finger tips.

Plump sticky buds unfurl, and bring
Fresh light green leaves, to welcome Spring,
Flowers bloom next, pure white, not red,
One`s male, one`s female, so it`s said.

Branches beneath this splendid gown,
Gnarled and twisted, are darkest brown,
Seeking sunlight, filtering through,
If Summer`s breeze gives them a clue.

Then in September, we hear cries,
"Look big conkers, look at the size!"
Conkers are falling, everywhere,
Shiny, new, excitingly rare.

Once more, branches are all that`s left,
When Autumn winds make them bereft
Of orange, russet, brown and gold
Leaves, which in turn, release their hold.

As Winter`s frost steals through the air,
Stiff and brittle and starkly bare,
Each branch will wait with outstretched hand,
For Spring`s warm breeze, to heal the land.

THE OPEN DOOR

The countryman trudged with his dog
Across the moor, going through bog.
If he`d known then what was to be,
He would have walked more warily.

Rounding a Tor, he felt the need
To hurry forth with greater speed,
Black clouds like night loomed far ahead.
"We`ll try this stony track," he said.

They clambered down that track of stone,
Where sheep had often roamed alone,
Hurrying on as well they might,
Whilst daylight`s strength ebbed into night.

They reached a hut, hid on the moor,
`Twas left, long since, with open door,
He pushed it wide and entered in,
But what he saw, did pale his skin!

His dog, aware of what was wrong
Did cower low and whimper long,
His hackles rose, he growled, then howled
Towards the Tor, shrouded in cloud.

The man cried out, he wished they`d been
Far distant from this wretched scene.
He shivered now from cold and fear,
And called his dog towards him, near.

Strong wind and rain lashed at the door
Which flapped and banged, until it tore
From rusted hinges, flying free
From years of hanging, needlessly.

They turned and ran, whilst lightening flashed
Through sheets of rain, as thunder crashed.
Running in fear, from what they saw
When first they entered through that door!

Through troubled years he`d hardly speak
Of witnessing a sight so bleak,
But kept his dog close to his side,
Thus, they were found, the day he died.

AUNT MAUD'S DREAM

My Aunt's large, and also jolly,
A homely bird's Aunt Maud,
You'd never think her dream would be
To travel off abroad.

But she won a competition,
The rules said, she could go
To any distant far off place
For free, no cost, and so....

Her longed for dream could now come true,
Her passion for so long
To discover in the Far East,
The mystery of Hong Kong.

Eventually her ticket came
By special courier,
And when she saw it, Maud then knew
It really was for her!

At once becoming serious,
She thought, "I've got to slim,"
And so that she could board the plane
She tried out "Slim and Trim."

She spent the next months working hard,
Trying to change her weight,
So that the plane could leave the ground,
She left food on her plate.

Maud felt quite faint, but wouldn`t eat,
And it was sad to see
Someone who`d loved her food so much,
Not even drinking tea!

When she was due to leave UK,
It`s very sad to tell,
She was too weak to leave her bed,
Let alone leave the hotel.

Aunt Maud has learnt her lesson, now
She eats good food all day,
Next year she`s flying to Hong Kong,
She may do....well....she may!

SUPPOSING

Supposing that the world was square

And not round, as they say,

If you went out and walked too far

You might fall off one day!

A C R O S S   T H E   W O R L D

Morning comes. Time to travel on
Across the world to reach Hong Kong.
Five hours by coach and more by plane,
Weather`s fickle, sun first, then rain!

Monotonous, continuous, perpetual
Noise, in an
Overtaking, overtaken, overcrowded
Coach. There`s a
Holidaying, business making, all assorted
Bunch, off to
Exeter, then Bristol, then to Heathrow and then
Where? In this
Overtaking, overtaken, overcrowded
Coach, go the
Intellectual, intermingled, interesting
Bunch.

The airport looms and you arrive,
Surprisingly, you feel alive.
Hand in bags, show passport, get seat,
There`s even time for you to eat!

If you were home, you`d be in bed,
But now you board the plane instead.
You try to settle for the flight,
A seat is all you`ll have, tonight!

You watch a film then have a drink,
Do crosswords till your mind can`t think,
Your body sinks into deep pools,
As you reread the safety rules!

Then, quietly drifting into sleep,
With roaring noise within the deep
Recesses of your mind, you wake,
Finding still many miles to make!

More hours pass as in a dream,
Thoughts hang suspended, in a stream
Of silky liquid, eyelids close
To almost melt, as tiredness grows.

Slight turbulence brings sudden stress.
Jolted back into consciousness
You look around. Everything`s fine,
Food trolley comes, it`s time to dine!

Refreshed with food, not long to go
Before the blinds are raised, to show
Hong Kong, a world not seen before,
Though tired, you`re longing to explore.

WHAT TO DO (When you`ve got the time)

Pacify the fiercest wind, and tie with string that's strong,
Place it in an air-tight bag,
And rush it to
Hong Kong.

Look for a brilliant rainbow, and wrap it in clean straw,
Slide it in a golden box,
And send to
Singapore.

Just separate two snowflakes, and roll them in fine sand,
Glue them to a penny stamp,
And mail them to
Thailand.

Shovel up white crystal ice, and crush it with a bang,
Sieve it through a wire mesh,
And ship it to
Penang.

Parcel up some morning mist, with flowers dipped in dew,
Knot them with a silken thread,
And post them to
Peru.

Lay down six streaks of lightning, well underneath a rock,
Leave there, for the elements
To wire them to
Bangkok.

Bottle up clear glistening rain, and with the moon on high,
Sprinkle drops on passing clouds
Drifting towards
Dubai.

Catch twenty smiling sunbeams, and if there`s time left free,
Toss them to a twinkling star,
To shine on you
And me.

47

ISLES APART

Living every day in Hong Kong,
Looking out across the bay,
I think of things for which I long
From my home, that`s far away.

England`s fields grown lush with greenness,
Leaves quite wet with morning dew,
Orange pippins formed to fullness,
Pigeons flying down to you.
There, a wagtail, thrush and blackbird,
Robin, chaffinch and a jay
In the garden, so oft I`ve heard
Their dawn chorus, start the day.

Easter blooms in gay confusion,
Gathered for the village church,
Primroses, in gold profusion
Grown beneath the silver birch.
The smell of earth just after rain,
Red roses blushing with the dawn,
Daily, their perfumes would remain
To awaken us, each morn.

Throughout Autumn leaves keep falling,
Yellow, red and russet brown.
Why is England always calling
In her gentle topaz gown?
Frost and snow mixed in decanter,
After Autumn`s mellow wine,
Bringing Winter`s cold encounter,
Cannot change this heart of mine.

Here, buildings are quickly rising,
Glass and concrete, towering high,
Built so close, it`s not surprising
That we seldom see the sky!
Harbour waves steer junks and ferry,
Fishing boats of every kind,
On board families, so very
Strange from those I left behind.

Also daily, vessels sailing
In the harbour, to and fro,
Constant movement, never failing
As in shipping lanes they go.
On the far shore, tourists hustle
Through the busy crowded streets,
Searching in the noise and bustle,
Buying presents, gifts and treats.

Brightly coloured gems then glisten
On the velvet night-time air,
While I dreamily do listen
To the hub of night-time, where
Jewels shimmer in the distance
Mesmerizing me with light,
Stars though unseen, share existence
With this island of the night.

Will this island`s chest of treasures,
Paintings and calligraphy,
Draw me into lifelong pleasures,
Feeding creativity?

EVENING

An opaque creamy moon,
A rectangular room,
Beams of reds, blues, peeping through,
Sparkling jewels are
There, shining on you.

Oval droplets of light
Dancing round, shadows flight
Is swift, so fast, you can`t see
Brilliant colours are
Reflected on me.

Feel the warm curve of night
Mingling with evening light,
Bright diamonds surround.
Hidden shadows are
Nowhere to be found.

DAWN

The silver light of dawn, threads across the sky.

Quiet peaceful stillness.

Remembering, I sigh

Whilst thinking of my home.

Imagining, I fly

Back, to the very room

Where I used to lie.

Then a rosy glow and golden light appears,

The sun rises slowly,

Transparent through my tears.

The black kite circles close

Before she turns, then veers

Towards the Peak, her nest.

There she knows no fears.

TOO DARN HOT

My arms won't move
My legs are lead,
I'm rooted to the spot.
The reason why I feel like this
Is, it's too darn hot!

Don't feel like food,
Just want to drink,
Fresh apple juice, I've got.
I really wish it wasn't, but
Yes, it's too darn hot!

I can't get up,
I must lie down,
Wish I could sleep a lot,
Don't even want to walk one step,
For it's too darn hot!

I'd love to dance
On an ice-rink
Or sail off in a yacht,
To even thinks' impossible,
As it's too darn hot!

Switch on the fan
To make a breeze,
The air-con's gone to pot!
A small escape from humid heat,
When it's too darn hot!

Another verse?
No, I can't think,
The next line will be what?
But now you know the reason why,
`Cause, it's too darn hot!

QUESTIONS
AND
ADVICE
(To the flat above, on hearing a strange noise)

"Did you drop your dinner
On your polished floor?
I heard it through the ceiling.
So, did you get some more?"

"Were your beans good runners?
Did your peas go pop?
Did your bacon slither? So
What happened to your chop?"

When you`re eating next time
Tightly hold your plate.
Or, the food you`d like to eat
Won`t be the food you ate!

FLIGHT FROM HK

"Good evening Sir, please come this way,
We have to leave without delay.
Departure time, is ten past nine,
And from Hong Kong the weather`s fine.
Don`t worry, all will be OK,
So just relax Sir that you may
Enjoy the films, and tasty food,
Our tea is always freshly brewed.
All alcoholic drinks are free,
And after meals, we serve coffee."

"Please kindly watch, whilst I display
The life-jacket and safest way
It`s used, in an emergency.
Remember, we fly over sea.
That will be all, except take care,
Make sure your belt is fastened, there.
We hope you have a pleasant flight,
And get some sleep during the night,
Then feel refreshed when you arrive
In London, at five thirty-five!"

PEOPLE WHO SNORE

People who snore
Are such a bore.
There should be a law
Against it!

People who snore
Don`t care a straw,
Say, "Luck of the draw,
Can`t help it."

People who snore
Should shut their door,
And sleep on the floor
To stop it.

People who snore
At twenty, or
When they`re ninety four,
Still do it.

People who snore,
I`m really sure
Cannot just ignore
They do it.

People who snore
Can`t hear their roar,
We can, and implore
"Don`t do it."

People who snore,
Get help before
You all start a war!
Please stop it.

But here`s the score,
Millions galore
Whether rich or poor,
All do it!

FRED

I knew a man whose name was Fred
Who hardly ever left his bed,
For, out of bed, unprotected,
Accidents he just collected.

The danger was in poor Fred`s feet,
Which frightened off most folk he`d meet,
As tripping on dripping laces,
Left him sprawling in their faces.

When he turned right, he would forget,
Look back, and slip on something wet.
Or, turning left, he`d circle round
Too far, then trip, as he unwound.

Fred`s dancing was, sort of, abuse,
"Ouch!" Two left feet was his excuse!
His dance steps, no one could decode,
Quite puzzling at his prancing mode.

And so poor Fred went through his life
Misunderstood, and causing strife.
With bumps and bruises, broken bones,
Doctors, hospitals, moans and groans.

Then falling hard on his behind
Made Fred sit up, and change his mind.
Loudly he said, "I`ve had enough
Of accidental falls and stuff."

And so the safest place for Fred
Turned out to be, a double bed.
He spent the rest of his long life
Right there, tucked up with his dear wife!

A NONSENSICAL DAY

When gallivanting` off one day
I chanced `pon my Aunt Maud on way,
An` knowin` that she`d like to chat,
I stepped aside, an` doffed me `at.
"Ow be ee, Jack?" she cried, with smile,
"Fair to middlin` Aunt Maud." An` while
She nattered on `bout this an` that
I started like, to eat me `at!
I soon found out it tasted good,
So tired of standin` where I stood,
I knelt down right low, `pon one knee,
An` eatin` now so fast you see
I couldn`t stop, an` grew real big,
Lookin` just like me Uncle`s pig!
I could not move now, up or round,
I was stuck fast, there on the ground.
Aunt Maud tried `ard with `elpful `and
To raise me up so I could stand.
But, I was stuck there `pon that spot,
An` might `ave died, if I `ad not
Decided I would eat NO MORE!
Aunt Maud said, "Jack, I`ll fetch the law."
She came back with a coil of rope,
Plus, eight strong men, so there was `ope
Of standin` me upright again.
I `eard `em countin` up to ten,
"`OLD ON TO ROPE!" The next I knew
The sky was closer, as I flew
Over their `eads, an` on beyond,
SPLASH! I landed in Uncle`s pond!

So take advice, don`t overeat,
Or else like me, you`ll get wet feet!

HOW TO SLIM

Just purse your lips
At deep fried chips,
Grilled bacon slice
Is very nice,
But leave behind
All fat and rind.
White meat is best,
Cook chicken breast.
Be sure to eat
Only lean meat.
Make half, not whole
Toad-in-the-hole.
Poach a fresh fish
For a light dish.

Wake up, don`t dream
Of clotted cream,
Or how to bake
Another cake,
And do not cut
A jam doughnut.
Tie up your box
Of chocs, with locks.
Avert your eyes
From custard pies.
Have strawberries
With ripe cherries,
Enjoy stewed pear,
Not an éclair.

Never mutter
"I want butter,"
Eat all your bread
With low fat spread.
For hunger`s pang
Avoid meringue,
Instead just munch
Salad, for lunch.
In a food shop
Know when to stop.
First, make a list,
Be firm, resist.
For a surprise,
Try exercise,

If all this fails,
Alter your scales!

THE TRAIN BY ORCHARD LANE

Aunt Maud had got to catch a train
So hurried off in pouring rain,
She had to catch the half past two
And now the time was quarter to.

Thinking she'd lots of time to spare
She didn`t cut across the Square,
Unfortunately for Aunt Maud,
As seconds saved, could have been stored.

A stranger stopped and asked the way,
Wanting to chat, this caused delay,
Then rushing off Maud tripped and fell,
Letting out one stupendous yell!

The stranger came back full of care
And sat Aunt Maud down, on a stair.
He listened to her tale of woe,
Learning how far she had to go.

He tried to call a taxi cab
Aunt Maud thought this was really "fab!"
The answer came, "No cabs today,
Drivers on strike, wanting more pay."

Later, calmer and in less pain,
Aunt Maud thought she could walk again,
Thanking the man she said, "Goodbye,"
And set off for another try.

The time was now gone quarter past.
(How time does fly, how very fast
When we would like it to stand still),
Now, there was no more time to kill!

Aunt Maud had fifty yards to go
When wind and rain turned into snow!
Her umbrella wasn`t new
And now the wind just blew and blew.

She battled on, and with a shout
Watched her brolly turn inside out!
Staggering round the final bend
She hoped her nightmare would now end.

There was the station, and her train,
Just pulling out, by Orchard Lane!
Aunt Maud was thirty seconds late,
Barred, by the level crossing gate.

If Aunt Maud makes this trip again
She`ll go by car, and not by train,
And will not pass the time of day
With any strangers on the way!

ARE THERE?

Are there people around that really like kippers?

Are there some who love going fast on big dippers?

Are there students who never stop taking exams?

Though they`re quite able to convert ounces to grams!

Are there goldfish who`d rather not swim in a bowl?

Are there rabbits who don`t like to live down a hole?

Are there dogs that lie down and won`t go for a walk?

Are there talkative parrots that refuse to talk?

Are there husbands who retire, then never sit down?

Are there wives who get lost when they`re shopping in town?

Are there children who won't eat ice cream or jelly?

And possibly some who have never watched telly?

Are there folk who won`t travel by car, or by train?

Are there some who love walking for miles in the rain?

Are there answers to these questions?   Possibly, yes,

But I really don`t know, and I`d rather not guess!

THE RACE

The rush of wind, the speed, the thrill
Of racing down the steepest hill,
Yet, concentrating on the road
And hoping you`ve the lightest load.

This morning's early fresh air smell,
Brings memories, long gone, known well.
Dog walking, by a river bank,
Air nectar filled, dew laden, dank.

Now, you`re a cyclist, riding fast,
Gasping at air that's rushing past,
Holding on tight, whirling through space,
Knowing you have to win this race.

Tall trees flash by, you see a face
Remembered at some other place.
Ahead, crowds gather near the bend.
Friends will be waiting at the end.

So pedalling hard you make a move,
With aching arms, your legs must prove
You have the strength. Your chance you take,
Weaving, full pelt, and two lengths make!

In front at last! The hunting pack
Try to keep up, but pace they lack.
Excitement, fear, the end is near,
The cheering crowd is all you hear!

The marshal makes a special sign,
You realise you`ve crossed the line
But can`t believe the cup is yours,
With thanks, you fall down, on all fours!

ESCAPE

Twist, untangle,
Cut and run.
Slip and stumble,
Hearing gun.
Jump up quickly
Heart on fire,
Sun is sinking
Must not tire.
Leaping over
Fallen tree,
Broken branches
Grazing knee.
Stop the bleeding,
Eyes ablaze,
Search horizon
Through this maze.
Distant voices,
Must keep still,
Hide in shadows,
Rest, until
Feeling stronger
Without pain,
Then escape, and

FREEDOM GAIN!

WHITE HORSES

White horses dance on silver seas,
While surfers chance their luck, and seize
Their moment, catch a wave, and ride
On top, and with the rushing tide.

Surfing the waves with massive swell,
Feeling the thrill when all goes well,
Not minding if the sea is rough.
To catch one wave, is not enough.

Watery sprays, fast moving sea,
Holding on tight, but feeling free,
Flying at speed then dipping low
Twisting and turning, till they slow.

Another wave, no one can tell,
If they will catch this one as well,
Till gracefully, they proudly stand
Surfing swiftly, towards the land.

THE HARBOUR

Small boats that shine in harbour brine,
Touching fenders, feeling free,
Let cool water lap their loose line,
Safely sheltered, by the quay.

Seagull sentries at attention,
Sleek and smart, in bright sunlight,
Alert, without hesitation
All at once are gone, in flight.

At dusk, lights reflected, glisten
Through dark depths of coloured sea,
Jewels shimmer, as we listen
To this hushed serenity.

DEPARTURE

Clouds suspended in the sky
Hang crowded overhead,
Forever slowly changing
To make an angel`s bed.

White yachts rock on the water,
Old dinghies nudge the bank
Where the mist moves silently,
Through still air, cold and dank.

Silver light heralds the morn,
It dazzles those who look
Across the glistening water.
Whilst others, read their book.

Greased engines start to rumble,
Creased sleepy faces yawn,
Countless years, perhaps, since they
Have left their beds, ere dawn.

The sturdy ship moves slowly,
Anchor and chains set free.
At last our journey has begun,
Into an unknown sea.

Passengers look up to gaze,
Intent, they close their book.
Out to crests of surging waves
Is where their eyes now look.

SOFT WAVES

Soft waves are pushing gently in
Against the rocks hard face,
Finding the cracks, they seep inside
Into a secret place.

Invisible, mysterious,
But soft waves hurry there,
Riding the surface of the sea,
As would a mermaid`s hair.

A precious second passes by
Before the waves rush out.
Whatever`s left behind them, is
Refreshed now, without doubt.

With constancy they`re organised,
Each moment, every day,
Rhythmically replenishing
All life around their bay.

At night, full circle shines the moon,
Reflecting light upon
The moving tide, yet still soft wave`s
Momentum carries on.

SHOWERS

Weakening sun did slide away,
Retreating shadows swept the ground,
As skies once blue, faded to grey
To let light showers fall all around.

Fresh showers sprinkled silver praise,
Wetting large jagged weathered rocks,
Unmovable in mountain`s haze,
Well seasoned, with these gentle shocks.

But showers, impatient, hurried on
To find another place to lay
Their shiny droplets, out upon
The valley`s wide and verdant bay.

As night approached more showers would soon
Spread out towards the distant shore,
Cast in bright light from the full moon,
Whose strength showed them a welcome door.

AWAY AT SEA

I did not know, I could not see
He who was far away at sea,
I did not sense, or feel the touch
Of hands on mine, held to entwine
For they were then with him, not me,
Away at sea, away at sea.

Then someone came and kissed my face,
And placed his arm around my waist,
I felt his warmth, his hairy beard,
No time, no need, to have it sheared.
But then he spoke, and said
"Sweetheart,
So sorry that we`ve been apart."

"Who is it dear, who is it dear?"
Pretending that I couldn`t hear
Those words, slowly I shook my head,
But would it matter what I said?

Out of the blue,
Dropped like a bomb!
I called my father
"Uncle Tom."

He that came from sea and ships
Heard these words come from my lips.
He sighed and wept to hear me say
I did not know him, on that day,
Known by his wife, and by his son,
I was unsure of what I`d done.
Tears welled up, I turned and fled,
To hide in blankets, on my bed.

To me it was a mystery,
My father here, how could it be?
When they had always said to me,
"Away at sea, away at sea."

REMEMBRANCE

On my arrival the music started,
How could I possibly feel downhearted?
I walked to the steps as proud as a queen,
Wondering if anyone else had seen
My grand arrival, or heard this great sound,
But, I was alone, as I looked around.

So I climbed the steps, but then near the top
My heart jumped a beat, I just had to stop.
Was it an orchestra playing so loud?
Why was I feeling so regal and proud?
As I reached the door, a girl let me in,
"Name? Dentist? Sit down," she said, with a grin.

I sat. All at once the music ended.
Sitting there, I no longer pretended
That I was special, it wasn`t for me.
But who was it for? So where could they be?
The invisible musicians, whose tune
Had stopped as soon as I entered that room.

I tried to relax, then with treatment done
I swept through the door, and started to run.

As I flew down the steps, medals of gold
Worn by brave gentlemen, upright and old,
Shone in the sunshine, worn proudly for those
Who had died in two wars, because they chose
To fight for their country, for me and you.
The fanfare was for them, at last I knew.

I watched them march by, saw men who remain,
Rehearsing, re-living their youth again.
With courage etched on their wrinkled faces,
With eyes that have wept in distant places.
Their grief buried deep, their lives still go on,
But they`ll never forget, friends that have gone.

TIME

Time is more precious than pure gold.

Time seems so endless when we`re young,
Our lives are new, our songs unsung.
Like birds, we test our wings, and learn
Which way to fly, which way to turn.
More years ahead, than are behind,
Gives freedom, and an open mind
To think, with exploration, through
Distant horizons veiled view.
Soon, songs unsung we start to sing,
Their changing rhythms, everything
Mixing our days, weeks, months and years,
With joyful notes, laughter, with tears.

Horizon`s glow now shows the way
For evening light to follow day.
But, with each setting sun, we`ve grown
So fast, the years have simply flown.
We then remember being told,
"Time is more precious than pure gold."
Wound up, and spinning like a top,
Remembering in time......we stop.
And as we stop, time stands still too,
So giving us time, to review
Our memories, and all we`ve done
Together, with the setting sun.

FROM FIRST TO LAST

First line implies
Truly, surprise!
A story that will freeze,
Then melt, a heart
Broken apart.
I do hope it will please.

I mow the lawn,
Find feathers torn,
Poor creature, flown from life.
Then fill the seed
For birds that feed
Not needing fork or knife.

In a flurry
Cook the curry,
Put dishes in the sink.
Knowing I`ll get
Fresh thoughts, to let
My pen dip in the ink.

Middle lines come,
And I have fun
Juggling them about.
After a while
A rhyme with style
Quite suddenly, jumps out!

I`ve dried each plate,
It`s getting late,
And everyone `s been fed.
With bedtime past
The line that`s last,
Will have to stay unsaid!

Carol has lived most of her married life in Devon, and spent almost a decade in the Far East with her husband and four children.

For the past five years Carol has been Poet in Residence for Mayfield Association, producing two poems each year for their newsletter, and some of her poems have appeared in other publications.

Living near the coast Carol followed progress and became a sponsor of Team Phillips, the catamaran built at Totnes for Pete Goss, and when Pete sailed to Australia on Spirit of Mystery, Carol wrote a poem which appeared on his web site in February 2009.

Apart from her grandchildren and her love of dogs, Carol`s other interests include gardening, growing and photographing flowers, drawing, dance and theatre. She hopes this little book will give all its readers *A Magic Time.*